Culture Craft: Change in a Jiffy

An Organisational Change Story

A. W. Jones

Foreword

Theories of organisational culture are well established. The works of Edgar Schein during 1980s began an awakening. Corporations began to understand their culture and tried to decipher the cultures of their competitors. Implicitly Executives knew that 'good' cultures were common in successful companies and 'bad' cultures presided in those that failed, but the formula was not easily transferable. In time more culture models were developed and further research was conducted. Culture now features prominently on the business school agenda. However, many Managers and

Executives still lack the toolkit to change a culture. This book is a story to help leaders, change agents, students and public servants to learn about organisational culture and to offer practical guidance on how to apply culture change.

In recent time any industry or company that fails or suffers a scandal is branded as having a 'toxic' culture. This description had a double intent of blaming the Executives, who should know better and absolving the Managers lower down, who are deemed as powerless to have acted as the culture was working against them. This is of course a misrepresentation. While Executives have ultimate fiduciary power the power and responsibility to manage culture is distributed throughout the organisation. Everyone has a role to play. Managers and employees need to understand and harness their role in building the right culture.

Culture Craft is the story of Jiffy, a company in need of some change. Jiffy is fictional, however the challenges and series of events in the story are borrowed from far and wide, across industry and organisation type, to represent the difficulties many companies experience whilst changing culture in the real world. The reader will hopefully recognise these challenges and will no doubt sympathise with the team at Jiffy. The author hopes that this story provides the reader with a memorable parable about how to change culture 'in a jiffy'.

Chapter 1

Jiffy

Jim was playing golf. The game was going well, the regular practice was paying off. It was 2pm on a Thursday, but he had the time to play. No need to return to the office anytime soon. Jim made sure that Fiona kept his diary open on Thursday afternoons to prevent any need to rush back. As CEO it was his prerogative to make time for relaxation and reflection, at least that's how he justified it to himself. Jim's muscular bulk hammered the ball down around the course. A bulk that betrayed a lifetime of manual work. Now that he wasn't doing as much the bulk was turning soft. Golf was the closest thing Jim got to a hard day now, he hadn't touched a factory tool in years.

Jim's golf outings were always shown as 'Meetings' in the Executive calendar, but everyone knew what they were. "When did Jim ever go to a meeting by himself these days?" Fiona muttered to herself, a little tired of the need to pretend Jim was somewhere else.

The rest of the Execs cut Jim plenty of slack. After founding the company 25 years ago 'from nothing', as they were often reminded by Jim, he deserved some down-time. Retirement was still some way off, but he deserved a gentle glidepath into his later years. Jim still cared deeply about his company, but he was handing over more and more responsibility each year to his Executive team, he had hand-picked them to carry-on the firm and he trusted them with it.

The company made timber products, primarily component parts for other companies, such as chair legs for fabric sofas and handles for garden tools. Of course times had changed. When Jim began he was a carpenter in the local furniture factory. Later Jim set-up his own small workshop along with a few of the older shop stewards. They made dining furniture, sideboards and even rocking chairs. They had a passion for craftsmanship.

These were the first product lines of the firm, granting the company a reputation for quality at competitive prices. The company name evolved at this time, from Jim's Furniture Factory (as it was initially known) into JFF, sometimes known as Jiffy. A name that stuck when Jim and the initial team spent weekends and evenings meeting additional and short-notice orders to keep their clients happy - they were done 'in a jiffy'.

JFF managed through some tough times. Improving mass-production techniques drove the market in two directions, bespoke and high quality at the top end and lower quality machine only at the bottom end, which often used poorer quality timber. Increasing imports from competing countries with lower costs also made it hard to differentiate on price.

The strategy of the past had changed, JFF played to it's strengths and focussed on craftsmanship and strong operational performance. In time finding a steady market in those component timber parts for locally made furniture and tools. Jiffy's clients valued the quality and the finish of the products. Over a few decades the company grew, the initial workshop became a factory, one manager changed into a dozen and a few customers turned into more than twenty strategic partnerships across the country and some beyond. Despite the company's growing number of employees new joiners soon learned that JFF stood for *'solid wood, made to specification, in the spirit of a proud craftsman'*. A mantra Jim would often repeat out of habit when talking to employees and customers.

Chapter 2

COO

Greg was new to JFF. An experienced middle manager, Greg had relocated to the area and had met Jim when joining the golf club. After a few rounds of golf together Jim made Greg an offer to come and work at JFF as Chief Operations Officer, a new role that took on responsibilities that were previously part of Jim's remit, but which he wanted to step-back from. Even though Greg didn't know the industry Jim was confident that his broad management experience would be an asset to the team, plus Jim thought it was probably time to hire an 'outsider'. His Executive team had become too comfortable and inwardly focused, so he wanted to bring in a fresh perspective. "Welcome to the Jiffy family" he said when Greg accepted.

Greg spent his first months working with Jim and the other Executives to understand the business, the industry and JFF's relative performance. The role was essentially a go-between for the Factory, located out of town and the head office where the Executives, Sales and Finance teams were based. This gave Greg the critical responsibility of communicating the overall strategy to the production and design teams at the Factory, as well as reporting back with any feedback from sales and marketing. In reverse, Greg was also the conduit for communicating factory operational performance, design team ideas and inventory challenges to head office.

Greg's first challenge was dealing with Brian. As Factory Manager, Brian was essentially head of production and design, he was an old friend of Jim's, having been one of the few that followed Jim from the local factory to start JFF. Brian could be difficult to deal with. Greg had been forewarned by other Executives, but soon learned himself of Brian's obstinance when he refused to give Greg access to the factory until Jim provided written approval. A petty and useless act seemingly derived from Brain's insecurity and determination to stop "Head Office pen pushers from interfering in my factory", as re-told it to the factory Foremen over coffee, having a good laugh.

A further complication was that even though Greg was COO, the Factory Manager continued to report directly to Jim. "As Brian is an old friend I don't feel comfortable asking him to report to you as the new COO, not yet at least" Jim explained "We can review the situation further down the road". They would have to work together and 'influence' each other, Greg recalled from working in other 'matrix' organisations. The title of COO was mostly honorific he realised.

It seems that Brian's personality and management approach didn't only have an impact on Greg and the other Executives. Staff turnover at the factory was getting worse. The Designers found Brian's refusal to sanction even the smallest of expenditures infuriating and were left feeling unappreciated. One of them had left and was enticing some of the others to leave too. "There are more interesting design jobs than spade handles and chair legs" the Designer had said to Jane, head of HR, who related it to Greg later. During the exit interview the Designer admitted that she enjoyed working close to home and appreciated the respect she received locally for working at Jiffy. But found that Brian's wearisome management style was too much. She added that it was beginning to weigh against the rest of the design team too, although they probably wouldn't admit it to HR.

The same was true for the carpenters and machine operators, many joined with hopes of building the skills of a master craftsman, but although JFF resisted some elements of mechanisation it was inevitable that more and more tasks were being carried out by machines. The carpenters became operators, little more than automatons moving pieces of wood in and out of saws and milling machines, rather than making something themselves by hand. After a few years the new joiners would leave, their dreams unrealised.

A further challenge, beyond the factory, was the bottom line. Greg had reviewed the numbers with Susan, the CFO. Year after year margins were being squeezed by rising costs and customers demanding more competitive rates. Some of JFF's key customers had consolidated over the years, increasing their bargaining power and leaving JFF as price takers; they could not afford to turn down the business. The head of Sales, Mike justified "something is better than nothing, even if the margin is negligible". Mike would leave it to Brian to make it work, "he always manages to shave a bit more cost out of the factory" he added in a rare gesture of respect.

Greg raised his concerns about the margins and the factory to Jim over a beer in the Club

House, practically the only place Greg could get a meeting with Jim these days. Jim's response was telling, "I know the way ahead will be tough, and frankly I don't have the energy to keep fighting these battles". Jim was looking down as he made this confession. Saying it out loud had crystalised the thought and it made Jim feel guilty. As if he had betrayed his colleagues and customers. Jim was quiet for a long time. Greg felt uncomfortable.

Finally, Greg broke the silence, "do you want me to take the lead in turning things around?". Jim agreed with a nod then left. Later that evening Jim sent an email to the Executives:

To: Executive Team
From: Jim
Subject: Holiday

Execs,

Going on an extended holiday. Greg will be leading some strategic initiatives, please give him your support. No changes to existing authorities at this time.

See you in a few months.
Jim

Chapter 3

Executive Meeting

There was plenty of gossip the next day about Jim's email. It seems it had quickly leaked out and JFF was full of speculation. Greg played down the situation and quietly invited the Executives to a meeting off-site to not attract too much attention. The uncertainty over Jim's holiday must have been significant, it even motivated Brian to leave the factory to attend the meeting. Mike from Sales and Susan from Finance joined too, along with Jane from HR,

Tim from IT and Fiona the Executive Assistant, who without Jim around had more time and was taking notes.

Greg began by recounting his conversation with Jim the previous evening, and by asking for their feedback on the challenges facing the company. It started civilly, but soon there was some snarky comments and finger pointing as Executives shifted blame around. Brian blamed Mike for selling too cheap, Jane blamed Brian for creating a toxic workplace at the factory creating more HR workload, Susan was blamed for the rising cost of raw materials, even though inventory procurement was actually part of the factory, but her team paid the invoices. Fiona broke the tension by announcing the arrival of tea and coffee.

Greg stood by the flipchart, he knew that JFF needed a root and branch review of it's strategy. As the rest sipped their drinks he drew a line down the centre of the page. The left hand column was labelled 'problems', the right hand side was left unlabelled. Greg asked the team to repeat their complaints by shouting out the issues they faced. One by one they came, this time more coherently as the team realised they were in it together: "Rising costs", "falling margins", "staff turnover", went up quickly. Some more personal items followed and were encouraged by Greg even though they seemed trivial: "Not enough parking spaces at head office", "too much email", "bad coffee", "no tea trolley", "Christmas party was cheap and nasty". Greg put them all up on the flipchart. Acknowledging their need to vent.

Something was missing, Greg tried to lead the group but got nowhere. Finally he wrote it down: "Jim is asleep at the wheel". There was an audible gasp, everyone looked insulted. Jim was a friend, father figure and boss. He'd grown the company 'from nothing' and was the embodiment of his slogan '*solid wood, made to specification, in the spirit of a proud craftsman*'. In stark contrast Greg was an unappreciative outsider, "who was he to judge" they thought "Jim gives him a job and then he stabs him in the back". Greg knew he had gone too far, he always did have a way of being too blunt. The room was quiet until someone mumbled an insult under their breath. Brian walked out. The others followed. Only Susan, the CFO remained.

"I agree with you", she said. Susan had seen the decline in the company in black and white, the numbers got worse with every subsequent accounting period. "Changes are required and fast, Jiffy will be broke before the end of the year at this rate", Susan shared the grim forecast. But without the authority to make changes Greg and Susan agreed they were going to struggle to make a difference.

Until they considered the things they could change. Greg was reminded of a seminar he'd attended about Corporate Culture at a recent conference. What had struck him was how the small things can make a difference, in fact some of the smallest things can make the biggest differences. Greg looked up some of the culture models and began making notes. He shared them with Susan. "What do you think are the key elements of JFF's culture?"

Susan wrote them out on the next flipchart page:

- *Jim as the soul of JFF (Greg insisted on including this after the reaction during the meeting)*

- *Resisting mechanisation in favour of craftsmanship*

- *Using solid wood*

- *Proud local business*

Greg and Susan stared at the list and reflected if it was accurate, they tried to summarise the list into a statement and found themselves repeating Jim's motto *'solid wood, made to specification, in the spirit of a proud craftsman'.* Jim had said it best all along, even new joiners and our customers knew the motto, so what was wrong with it? If that was a statement of the JFF culture what would they have to change?

Susan and Greg referred back to the flipchart and headed the right hand column 'Solutions'. They tried to complete the exercise.

Problems	Solutions
Rising costs	Cost appropriate to people and product
Falling margins	New products, niches, higher value
Staff turnover	Improved working environment, meet aspirations
Not enough parking spaces at head office	Ride share??
Too much email	?
Bad coffee	Look into new coffee provider
No tea trolley	Time machine?
Christmas party was cheap and nasty	Review budget
Jim is asleep at the wheel	New CEO....?

They weren't impressed with their efforts to find solutions, they were very generic and some didn't even have any solutions. Some were jokes to let off steam, like the 'time machine', "who expects a tea trolley in this day and age" Greg had said exasperated. Susan began a new more productive train of thought. "There is obviously a problem with making money, that is a straight and brutal equation, money in minus money out. I don't feel comfortable spending more on coffee and parties until we fix that". Greg agreed. They decided that getting the right products, positioning and pricing was going to be key, but they needed the rest of the team to work that out, perhaps even more people. The whole of JFF might be needed to create solutions to these problems.

That gave Greg an idea, "let's use the culture to solve the problem", Susan didn't catch-on, "*how does 'solid wood, made to specification, in the spirit of a proud craftsman'*" solve problems?".

"It doesn't" Greg added, "it has the right intent. But we need a new statement, something that points to our need for new customers, our need to innovate and our desire to evolve". Susan burst into laughter "You sound like a Management Consultant" she said derisively. Greg smirked in agreement. He wrote down in plain english what JFF needed:

- Products with higher margins

- Control of costs

- To retain staff

- Committed leadership

Greg reflected on the list. If these were achieved JFF would be much more certain of a safe future. He combined them with the original motto, the new culture statement read:

"JFF seeks out new customers and crafts solid wood products to meet their needs. Everyone at JFF assumes leadership for controlling costs and looking after our people".

Not as snappy as Jim's motto, but it was true to the original and was simple to communicate. Susan endorsed it and said she would speak to the other Executives to get them onboard.

Chapter 4

Artefacts

The culture models Greg had referred to listed some very visible indicators of culture, the symbols and artefacts of the organisation. When Greg returned to the office he looked around and tried to remember what it was like on his first day. What had occurred to him then that made JFF unique.

There were some real tangible items, status symbols like the Executive offices and priority parking spaces. Trademarks and logos on the stationary, signage and pens. Greg reflected that changing these items wouldn't really have an impact on customers or product design, even though they were an easy choice. There was nothing about these in the culture statement.

After driving over to the Factory Greg continued to search for visible artefacts of the JFF culture. He admired the hard assets and machinery there. The resistance to increasing the number and sophistication of these machines were significant. Some of the machines looked as old as Jim, but he realised that was the point. The more traditional ways were what JFF was about. That's what made JFF known to its customers; opting for traditional craftsmanship over machination and automation.

Greg waited to meet with Brian, he didn't want to barge in and assert his authority. Frankly he didn't have much authority anyway, but after the meeting where he insulted the aura of Jim by claiming he was 'asleep at the wheel' (later admitting to himself it was a poor choice of words), Greg decided not to force the issue and kept waiting.

The waiting area in the factory consisted of a small seating area outside of Brian's office. The Designers shared an office next to Brian's, most of their desks were empty. Both offices were on the upper floor of a two storey office building, which was connected to the factory, a larger building that resembled an aircraft hanger.

After waiting more than a quarter of an hour Greg realised that Brian wasn't going to see him anytime soon and so he took a walk around the office building. The lower level housed a changing area, lunchroom, storerooms, a large training room and a lobby area. Greg could hear the noise of machinery and snippets of some friendly banter between the Operators in the adjoining factory. He thought he heard something about "golf meeting".

On the wall in the lobby he saw a large framed photograph of Jim, Brian and the other initial JFF carpenters, it was taken outside an older, smaller workshop. Some of the carpenters were sitting on rocking chairs. In the background the large workshop doors had a painted sign on them saying 'Ready in a Jiffy'. They all looked tired but pleased with themselves, perhaps they had just completed one of their legendary 'all-nighters' to make up an order for an important client.

Greg noticed that the picture was on the wall next to the 'punch-clock', which was actually a modern device using fingerprints. All of the operators would pass this each day when 'clocking in'. Greg smiled and reflected that Brian was no stranger to creating a culture. He returned to the second floor with an idea brewing.

Finally Brian invited him into his office, looking a bit pleased with himself after making Greg wait more than an hour. He mentioned that Susan had called and explained about the desire to adopt a new culture, he was open to the idea. Brian didn't want to see the company he had built alongside Jim collapse into bankruptcy, Susan's insistence of a less than twelve month runway was enough to shake him into action.

Greg was pleased to hear Brian was conducive to change and felt that they had turned a corner professionally during their chat. Greg realised that being on Brian's own turf had made him more comfortable, making him wait also helped to inflate his ego and changed the power dynamic between them. "Brian was important" Greg thought, "not just to himself, but as a symbol of JFF too". On his way out after the meeting Greg had one final question for Brian "Can I borrow the photograph by the punch-clock?"

Chapter 5

Power

Feeling a little more optimistic about the task at hand Greg returned to Head Office. He continued to dwell on the symbolic nature of the photograph. Walking into the bright and airy office building Greg saw the brutal contrast between Head Office and the Factory. The memory in the photo was lost in this building. If it was posted in the office lobby it would look out of place, inconsistent. Greg resolved that the factory itself was a symbol of JFF, it was more appropriate, more consistent with the past. It was a local institution and people were proud to get a job there, until they found out the job wasn't the same one their friends and relatives had worked a generation before.

Greg was also happy he had found some common ground with Brian and that his short-term reputation as Jim's potential usurper or as a back-stabber was receding. Thinking again about the culture seminar Greg was reminded that those with power had a significant impact on culture. Not only the formal lines of authority, but the real power; who has the ability to shift the way things are done?

Greg worked it through in his head. Jim was obviously powerful, if he ever came to the office anymore people would follow his lead, but that vacuum was unfilled for now. The other Execs held power, both formal and informal. Susan was clearly a good influencer, she had won Brian over and was hopefully doing the same with the others. What about Brian, how much power did he have?

Greg was torn on the answer. Brian clearly ran the whole factory and even found routine savings and optimisations through his know-how and support from his team. The Operators seemed happy enough, despite the general engagement trend being downward. The Designers were less happy, as shown by their absenteeism and one recent resignation. His power was split Greg resolved, the Operators respected him but the Designers saw him as an obstacle.

The other departments were less clear, Greg asked Jane from HR, Tim from IT and Mike from Sales for a coffee, not disclosing why. They decided to go to the cafe down the street to get some privacy and because the coffee was delicious, well at least compared to the office coffee. Greg could sense that they were more receptive to him now, he guessed that Susan had worked her magic again.

Greg opened with a provoking question, addressed to them all "Are you powerful?". They all looked at him suspiciously, he could feel the figurative shutters coming down, they were about to class him as an outsider again, undoing Susan's good work. He quickly clarified "What I mean is, when you need to get something done, especially something outside of your department, can you do it?".

Tim was first to jump in, it appears he had a bit of an axe to grind "not really", he said. "Everyone comes to me when they have a problem with their computer or the factory guys complain when one of the control systems on the machinery freezes up, and I have to jump to it, but when I need to do some preventative upgrading or server maintenance no one wants to listen". Greg made a note and looked at Mike.

Mike looked uncomfortable, looked away and then back at Greg. "You remember what I said last week about Brian. He often puts limitations on what the Designers can do, either from material selection or cost, that can get in the way. I appreciate he's under pressure to keep costs down, but it's limiting my Sales teams. I don't have much power to change things there".

Jane was less confrontational "I feel powerful enough to do my job, I can manage the day to day, hiring isn't too difficult as people are attracted to work at Jiffy, it's the overall situation that makes me feel powerless. People are concerned about the direction the company is going in and Jim's email has made it worse. I want to improve engagement but it's challenging when you can't pay more or fund parties or buy nice tea and coffee" Jane finished looking into her cup.

"Do those things make people more engaged?" Mike challenged. "My salespeople are excited about growth, about challenging targets and about working for Jiffy". He smiled "In fact, here's a funny one for you. One of my top Reps took his kids to the swimming pool the other day and overheard someone talking on the phone in the changing rooms, something about dreading going to IKEA later on with his wife to buy furniture. My Rep waited for him to finish his call then struck up a conversation with the guy, sympathising about being dragged around IKEA and giving him a sales pitch about buying solid wood furniture, just like Jiffy used to make. Apparently the other guy practically ran out of there".

"Why?" Jane asked.

"Because my Rep was stark naked at the time!", Mike leaned back laughing. "His new name amongst the other Reps is 'the Naked Salesman'". The others joined in the laughter, pleased to hear a jovial work story for a change.

Chapter 6

Changes

Greg sat in his office in deep thought. He doodled the summary of JFFs culture *'solid wood, made to specification, in the spirit of a proud craftsman'*. Thinking about the validity of that statement. All of the things he had heard about people leaving the organisation, not just Designers, some Operators too, didn't resonate with that culture. They weren't proud craftsmen. In fact they were let down by the lack of craftsmanship. The culture was mis-sold to them and they became disengaged.

Alongside the old mantra Greg wrote the new aspirational strategy "JFF seeks out new customers and crafts solid wood products to meet their needs. Everyone at JFF assumes leadership for controlling costs and looking after our people".

Comparing the two Greg acknowledged that being a craftsman was important for JFF, or Jiffy as he'd have to start calling it, like everyone else. The craftsmanship was a differentiator, a selling point and a motivator.

Finding customers was also a culture change Greg realised. At the moment Jiffy was relying on a set of tried and trusted accounts, despite the efforts of 'the Naked Salesman' and the other Reps. Leadership was another gap, he admitted. Jim was asleep at the wheel, even though the phrase was disliked the effect was the same. Jiffy needed a leader to embody the new culture.

Greg walked down the hall and knocked on Jane's door, she welcomed him in. "I think we should make some organisational changes", he said.

'Okaaay', Jane drew out the accomodation to show some skepticism and but also a willingness to listen. "Tell me more", she added. Thinking that he didn't really have the authority for this.

"I know it's been this way forever, but some things are really out of place. Such as, I know the Designers need to be working closely with the factory, but they should be closer to Mike and the Sales team, let's move them to head office".

"But we tried that years ago" protested Jane, "they spent so long on the road back and forth to the factory that it didn't work, even 'dotted line' reporting relationships into Sales and weekly team meetings didn't really stick. In the end we put it back as it was, with them reporting into Brian". Greg could see the logic, but pressed on. "What if we move Sales to the Factory?", Jane was wide eyed and incredulous. "And make Mike give up his office?"

"Yes" Greg concurred.

"That could work, as long as Mike agrees" Jane allowed cautiously. "Anything else?"

"In general, I think JFF, I mean Jiffy is too siloed. Sales stick with Sales, Design with Design, Operators with Operators, all the Executives do the talking and nobody else seems to really connect outside of their department".

"What can we do about that?" Jane asked.

"We need to build a culture of openness and communication. Everyone needs to take some responsibility, we all need to be leaders" Greg retorted, thinking of the second line of the new culture *'Everyone at JFF assumes leadership for controlling costs and looking after our people'*.

"Yes, but how? Jane persisted. Continuing his line of thought from before Greg spoke as soon as the light bulb lit up in his head "We should all move to the Factory".

Chapter 7

Moving

A few weeks later and the move was complete, albeit temporarily. The Executives had agreed to give it a three month trial. All of the head-office teams found space in the factory office building, cramming into shared offices and even putting desks into the waiting area. The place was buzzing.

The quick wins were tangible and intangible. Sales and Marketing teams were cohabiting with designers and so conversations were happening more easily, this led to a few product tweaks and some higher margin sales. They were working as team. Brian didn't mind the change of reporting line too much as the Design team were still next to him, and so he could check-in with them to ensure they didn't bend too much to the will of the Salesmen. Brian allowed his Operators and Foremen to do the same, asking them to visit the Sales, Marketing and Design office on a regular basis to ask questions and plan production, all in the spirit of the new culture. Furthermore the additional parking at the Factory made everyone happier about commuting to the new office, even though the coffee was still bad.

Susan had agreed with the landlord of Head Office for Jiffy to receive an almost complete credit for the three months of non-occupancy, on the proviso that the landlord could sublet the space to a neighbouring tenant who was having some renovations taking place in their current office space. Susan allocated some of the saved budget to the relocation and even had enough for a moving party - which was really an excuse to build some camaraderie between the teams that had been separate for so long.

The party took place during the weekend on a strip of grass inside the factory fence. A mobile pizza oven was brought in along with some beer, wine and soft drinks. A bouncy castle was hired and staff were encouraged to bring their families along. A makeshift stage was knocked-up by the Operators the previous day from off-cuts and spare material. Greg stood on it and was handed a microphone by Tim from IT. Greg was joined alongside by Mike from Sales, Susan the CFO and Jane from HR. Brian skulked to one side, off-stage.

Greg began "Welcome to the moving party, thank you all for coming and for bringing your families. I think you'll all agree that this factory is an institution. A symbol of Jiffy. I think it can be even more, a new way of working, a new home, perhaps a fresh start for a company that is looking a bit tired", Greg began to ramble. The crowd tensed up. Susan saved him by gently picking the mic out of his hand and redirecting the message "I think Greg is right. Jiffy is an institution, we've created products that are *solid wood, made to specification, in the spirit of a proud craftsman* for decades" The manta flowed easily for her. "But, there continues to be challenges, just like the past where Jim fought off pressure from imports and poor quality machined replicas, we continue to fight now. Our challenge this time is a shrinking market and evolving sales channels. Don't take it only from me, ask our very own Naked Salesman", a ripple of laughter spread through the crowd as they recalled the story of the Sales Rep in the changing rooms. They'd all heard it. The tension broke, the crowd relaxed and sipped their drinks in the pause.

"The move of Head Office teams to the factory" Susan continued, "embodies an initiative that Greg has been working on for some time. We need to make some changes, changes to how we work, what products we make and how we make them. Our new guiding motto will be *JFF seeks out new customers and crafts solid wood products to meet their needs. Everyone at JFF assumes leadership for controlling costs and looking after our people".*

Greg caught people staring at him, many of them with frowns. They didn't like the new motto. Susan gave a wan smile in the silence. Mike picked up the slack, using his powerful voice to project without the microphone. "I'm very excited and pleased about this change, Greg has done a fantastic job" the name check seemed to draw even more attention to Greg as he began to get physically smaller and somewhat retreated behind Susan. "This motto crystallizes a new way of working for Jiffy, it's not enough anymore to just make amazing products. Our products have to be built around our customer's needs, even if the customer doesn't know their own needs. We need to have greater reach, broader access and a more diversified customer base. This requires everyone to pitch-in. Perhaps not quite as much as our Naked Salesman" more sniggers "but he had the right idea" We're creating a culture where everyone plays a role in finding customers, suggesting products and controlling costs. That's the new way we're going to do things at Jiffy". There was a round of applause. Mike's authenticity had shown though, he really cared and wanted to keep Jiffy alive. Susan thanked Mike and asked everyone to have a good time, more details would follow on Monday.

Over the weekend Greg reviewed and redrafted his proposal for a new incentive programme. He knew that Control Systems were an indicator of culture, whether success was rewarded or failure penalised made a difference. How budgets were allocated and controlled was a signal of what was important to an organisation. How performance was ranked gave employees a measure of how to behave. These were all items that Greg had considered, but central to the new culture was seeking out new customers and distributed leadership on cost. He wanted to build a system to embody those values. He had already shared the key points with the other Execs, but wanted to make sure it was coherent and appropriate for the task, he knew this had to go well. The Execs had begun to warm to him, but his reputation amongst the rest of Jiffy wasn't good, the last thing he needed was to launch a half-baked initiative from 'Head Office'; that would be a backward step culturally.

On Monday Greg came in early. He hung a new picture on the wall of the training room, which now doubled as a conference room. It was a blown-up image of the photo he borrowed from the factory lobby. Younger versions of Jim, Brian and the others smiled back at him, the photo was a little grainy where the resolution wasn't quite good enough for the new size. Around the photo was a large white border. Printed on the bottom section of the border was the new motto in clear large text: "*JFF seeks out new customers and crafts solid wood products to meet their needs. Everyone at JFF assumes leadership for controlling costs and looking after our people*".

Greg sat with the others at the recently established Monday Morning Meeting, where all the Executives got together to review the week ahead. Something easy to do with everyone in one place, even Brian couldn't find a recurring excuse to miss it.

Jim had tended to have one on one meetings with his team, rarely gathering everyone together, this was part of the old culture, Jim at the centre and everyone else in orbit. That wasn't going to work at the new Jiffy, the team had to be interconnected, communicating more frequently.

Greg ran through the new incentive programme. It was broad and simple. Anyone could suggest a sales lead, a product or a cost saving item. All they had to do was send an email into a specific address with their suggestion. If that item resulted in more sales margin, a new customer or saved operational expense then the employee that recommended it got a share of the benefit. A formula was built in to the keep the system fair. 10% of cost saving or net margin went back to the organisation, half directly to the employee that recommended it and the remainder into a fund for the whole of Jiffy.

The Execs had some questions. "Sounds interesting" said Mike, "but who is going to check the amounts and make sure there's no fiddling of the numbers? For example a Sales Rep suggesting ways to sell more and then exaggerating the sales, or holding sales back and then making them later claiming they came from an idea he thought up?" Greg didn't have a full answer and was a little alarmed that this was Mike's first concern, "we can review items and overall progress in this weekly meeting, but I'm not sure about managing deliberate fraud, any ideas?", he opened it up to the group.

Susan jumped in "well Finance can check the amounts and make sure that we only reward actual savings or real additional profits". Mike answered part of his own question "ok, good, perhaps for Sales people we need someone to corroborate the improvement, and similar for Procurement people for costs savings, like a peer review and approval". Everyone looked less than convinced, it was already getting complicated.

Tim from IT had an idea after staring at the new picture on the wall with the motto at the bottom. "We need to live by our motto, he quoted '*Everyone at JFF assumes leadership for controlling costs*', we can publish the results on our intranet, let everyone see the submissions, the savings and the results. Transparency should be a keen motivator to do the right thing".

"What about the Operators?" said Brian. "They don't have access to computers here and so they can't send emails or see the intranet".

"Umm, I can hook up a monitor in the lunchroom with a scrolling list of the submissions, same as the website". Tim went on "As for sending in submissions, we can use a hard copy drop-box in the lobby, or they can send emails from home" Brian nodded and looked satisfied.

Susan raised an objection next "How are we going to pay out savings to employees, cash?"

"We can include additional payments to employees as bonuses through our payroll system" Jane chimed in. "But that will require some additional work on my side".

'It's still a bit complicated isn't it' Mike said "who is going to get the hard-copy slips out of the box in the lobby, do all of the compiling, put all of the emails into the database and so on?" Mike gestured with his hands wide apart "It's quite a lot of extra work". Greg explained that he'd already asked Fiona to take this on, she'd agreed willingly, happy for the extra responsibility and something consistent to work on now that Jim was on holiday, without any news of a return date.

Everyone agreed the action items, the incentive plan would be up and running in a week.

Chapter 8

Incentives

The incentive plan was a hit. Employees were submitting ideas on a regular basis. It started slowly, no one was really sure about making suggestions, they didn't want their 'silly idea' going up on the intranet. But one by one they came, first small and open ended without any real substance "IT training", "advertise our factory products online" then they became more robust "hold factory open days for prospective clients" and "competition for the best craftsmanship".

Fiona had some concerns and raised them to the Execs, "some of the suggestions are really similar, it's hard to allocate success to more than one person" The Execs agreed to review the suggestions that were similar each week and to rule in favour of one, the other or both, having a conversation with those involved if necessary. No one complained, most agreed to share the credit with someone else, especially as it was all for the greater good of Jiffy.

"There's another problem", Fiona added. "Someone has suggested 'Naked Salesman day' on a hardcopy slip, shall I actually put it on the list? It's obviously a joke, I'll leave it off". Greg weighed in. "No, better to put it on the list, we can't be seen to be policing ideas, and if we're too heavy handed with some light-hearted fun then people will stop contributing". Greg knew that breaking this new behaviour now would ruin the culture shift. Thinking of new clients and products had to become routine.

Jane looked concerned and then spoke up, "from an HR point of view having any reference to nakedness on our internal webpage isn't really appropriate, so we don't want to encourage that sort of thing". Brian broker a solution

"I have a fair idea who wrote that, I'll have a word with a few of the Operators to warn them against making racy suggestions in future, they'll take their lead from me on where the line should be drawn. Leave it up there for now as a reminder of what not to do".

"So when will it come down?" Jane asked.

"I've programmed the database to remove anything not verified or advanced after 45 days, that way employees don't get embarrassed by their suggestions that haven't worked." Tim answered. Jane looked relieved that it wouldn't be permanent.

"What about things that have worked, where do they go?" Greg enquired.

"They get moved to a separate list of 'completed items' on our server" said Tim.

"I think we should publish that list too, to remember and celebrate the good suggestions" offered Greg "perhaps a hardcopy in the waiting area, or even a leaderboard type of format with the ideas that generate the most value at the top".

The improvements were agreed and Fiona got to work making the changes with help from Tim. After a few more weeks the changes were in place, including an ideas leaderboard. The Execs agreed to have an award giving ceremony, which was a monthly gathering of all hands, held in the warehouse; the only indoor space capable of accommodating everyone. The first ceremony took place after only a week, a purposefully speedy timeline to build momentum to support the culture change by celebrating quick wins. It became a ritual, cake was served, people looked forward to it.

The Execs would read out the awardees for that month, explaining the suggestion, the action and the magnitude of the positive result. All the Execs shook hands with the employees who made the qualifying suggestions and certificates were handed out. Susan then unveiled the value in the employee fund. The pot was growing steadily as 5% of the cost savings or extra margin dribbled in. It already stood at enough for a better Christmas party, so that's what it would be put towards Susan announced, everyone cheered.

Chapter 9

Stories

A month later a new ritual was playing out. Two of the suggestions had been developed further and combined, the Craftsman competition and the customer Open Day. This way the clients could come and see the Jiffy facility, meet the team and could witness the capabilities of the Craftsmen.

The Craftsman competition had only one rule, "you can create anything; furniture, sculpture, homeware, anything" Brian has told them. Employees were free to use Jiffy facilities out of hours and without asking employees only used off-cuts and spare materials, rather than taking away from supplies destined for production. Not to be left out the designers also competed, submitting new prototypes both in hardcopy and on paper. One designer even developed a new mock website complete with new Jiffy logo. They were all welcomed.

After the Open Day employees were encouraged to vote for their favourite submission. Prizes were given for the top three, they were also exhibited in the lobby. A fantastic modern rocking chair won the top spot, drawing upon the Jiffy nostalgia it had no doubt won over the hearts of many long term employees, who were reminded of some of Jiffy's historical production runs. Second was a set of wooden toys; clever interconnecting blocks made of solid wood and finished to perfection. The mock-website and logo came third.

The employees were visibly pleased with the recognition and the spirit of the competition. They felt proud to be part of Jiffy and to be treated as Craftsmen rather than Operators. Jane made a note to change the official title of the role to Craftsman (or Craftswoman as needed) in the HR system. It was a small but symbolic step to reinforcing the culture of craftsmanship and improving overall employee engagement.

One of the clients who joined for the Open Day was very impressed with the competition. In fact the second place submission was seized upon as a potential product for a client of hers who had a chain of toy shops. Blocks that encouraged engineering skills were becoming increasingly popular and the fact that they were made from sustainable solid wood was a selling point to environmentally conscious parents. She would enquire with her client and then revert with feedback. Mike encouraged her to take the prototype as a sample and made some back of the envelope costings with Brian while she was on the phone. He presented her with some rough numbers and they agreed to talk the following week.

Jiffy was buzzing once again the following day, the story of the blocks being admired by a potential buyer was enough to create increased chatter around the coffee machine. This machine was in the waiting area outside Brian's office, the leaderboard of ideas was visible from there and there was speculation as to whether the blocks would make the top. That day more and more product ideas were submitted under the incentive plan.

The block story got Greg thinking about the culture model again. Stories were key to conveying information and teaching lessons. Humankind has always used storytelling as a way of passing on wisdom and communicating history. From cave paintings to fairy tales and Shakespeare people have used stories to create a memorable format to transfer knowledge. Cultures were made of stories. Greg knew that. Jiffy was changing it's story now, but they needed more to cement the new culture.

Greg asked Brian about the old days, the war stories, the all-nighters. Brian reminisced fondly. "In the past Jiffy was known for Jim and us, his crew. We worked all night, weekends, eighteen hours a shift sometimes" Greg shuddered at the breach of safe working practices, imagining the risk of being sleepy around some of the machinery. Brian reassured him "It was different then, fewer rules, but we looked after one another; told each other to rest or go home if we looked dangerous. It was all about being responsive to customer demand. Making amazing products out of a rusty old workshop". Greg reflected that this spirit had built a business despite tough competition, it grew it into a local institution.

But somewhere in the middle that story Jiffy lost it's way, Greg pondered afterwards. The factory tried to keep it going, which meant Brian tried to keep it going. Small touches like resisting more machinery and keeping the photo near the entrance, both were efforts to maintain the legacy. However, the weight of change told a new story.

The boss playing golf became the story. Brian being a miser became the story. Sales Teams selling too cheap and Executives living it up at Head Office with their parking space privileges became the story. People wanted to work at Jiffy, but after joining they left when they realised it wasn't what they expected, the real thing wasn't like the story anymore.

Greg was sipping a questionable cup of coffee as he saw Mike pick up the phone through the glass window that separated the Sales, Marketing and Design office from the waiting area. Mike made a motion to his team to keep the noise down by holding his hand out, palm down, moving his arm up and down as he held the phone with the other hand. A smile and then a frown came onto his face followed by a few more words and then the phone being put down. He rushed into Brian's office and grabbed Greg on the way round.

"We have the order from the toy shops" Mike confirmed. "5,000 units as an initial order. But we need to provide them in three days so that they can be shipped and marketed as part of their new STEM promotion which begins over half-term". He added warily. "If we can't do it on time they won't place the order. Can we do it?" He was looking at Brian, who had a twinkle in his eye.

Brian summoned his Foremen and the Craftsman who created the blocks up to his office. They discussed design, method and packaging, roping in Mike's Design and Marketing teams too. After two hours they had created four further prototypes, which refined the method and simplified the design, but left the initial idea and craftsmanship intact. The Design team had mocked up some simple cardboard packaging that they could get made locally in a few days.

The Foremen and the Craftsman who designed the blocks held training sessions for the other Craftsmen in the training room and on the factory floor. They started production and built up momentum, getting quicker with every batch. Someone got the pizza oven to come back to keep the craftsmen fed as they worked late. When the pizza chef wanted to go home Susan, Greg and Mike took turns making the pizza and serving, although to a much lower standard than the chef who had quickly taught them before going home.

Realising they had to up the pace the Foremen organised the Craftsmen into teams and allocated shifts, sending some home to rest. The factory would run all night to make the order.

Two more days continued this way. The order was met in time and to specification, in fact they'd made even more than required. Just like Jim used to say '*solid wood, made to specification, in the spirit of a true craftsman*'. After the order was shipped Brian gave all shifts the afternoon off and arranged for a spare set of the toys to be given to each employee. Greg kept an extra set and put them in lobby as a reminder of what was achieved.

"That's another story to add to the list" he thought.

Chapter 10

Living the new culture

Jiffy was flying now. It had only been a few months but the changes were making a huge difference. The income forecast had improved markedly due to orders of new products. Lower costs due to savings from employee suggestions were improving margins too. Susan confirmed in the weekly meeting that the survival timeline for Jiffy had improved from to more than eighteen months. Jane added that she had spent some time with the Design team and a sample of other employees to test engagement, "they are much happier now", she reassured the other Execs "No one admitted to wanting to leave Jiffy, which is a good sign, not definitive of course, but I got a sense that the new culture was giving them a new drive, a new sense of belonging".

The road ahead was still going to be tough Greg knew, but with an improved culture, where everyone was pitching in to find new ideas, new clients, new products and more savings it was looking hopeful that Jiffy would be a renewed success.

The Execs discussed a celebratory dinner in town for themselves to toast Greg's culture change initiative. Greg jumped in quickly "No, we can't do that".
"Why not?" Tim asked, who was looking forward to a night out.
"It's not consistent with the culture. If we begin to spend money on what could be perceived to be self-serving excess then we are repeating the mistakes of the past. We risk telling negative stories about ourselves through our own actions" Greg was determined to promote

and support the new culture. It was still fragile enough to break-down if it wasn't maintained.

"So what can we do to celebrate?" Mike enquired. "My Sales Reps have team dinners on a regular basis, it's important for them to meet and acknowledge their hard work. They share ideas and leads during those meetings. Spending time on the road is lonely for them and it's the only way for them to bond as a team."

"I'm not suggesting to change that Mike" Greg consoled. "That's a ritual your team has, it's tied to a justifiable reason and changing it would be a backward step. Provided the Reps follow the motto and take leadership over cost control they should be able to do the right thing by keeping their spending sensible. We need to role-model that behaviour too".

"We'll get everyone an extra drink at the Christmas party" Susan offered to Greg. "The employee fund keeps growing, so we should have enough for an extra glass or two. Let's celebrate our initial success then instead".

Fiona joined the Execs with a smile on her face. Everyone turned expectedly and Fiona shared the news "Jim is coming back!" she blurted out. "I just got off the phone with him, he's landing tomorrow. He asked me to request a short report back from all of you to get him back up to speed".

"Will be nice to see Jim again" Tim said unconvincingly. Mike nodded. Brian looked unsure, he certainly looked forward to catching up with his old pal, but he wasn't sure how Jim would react to the new Jiffy.

Greg began working on a presentation for Jim. More to order his thoughts than anything. He referred back to the key elements of the culture change initiative, listing them out:

- Moved Head Office into the Factory. Allowing Sales and Marketing to work closely with Designers and Operations. Breaking down silos across teams. Leaning on the symbol of the Jiffy factory as a lynchpin to unite the company.

- Launched the new incentive programme, sharing the expectation that everyone needs to work together to create leads, products and savings. Rewarding the right behaviours.

- Jane changed the title of Operator to Craftsman, a small gesture but one that put pride back into the role.

- Began the Craftsman competition, reviving the spirit of Jiffy and encouraging creativity and design.

- Held an Open Day for clients, a new ritual that was already leading to more sales. A chance for Craftsmen to showcase their work and for Jiffy's clients to meet the whole team.

- Established a routine Exec Monday Morning Meeting to ensure communication and to administer consistent management over drivers of the new culture, like the incentive programme. This helped to guide the changes coherently, rather than allowing inconsistent initiatives to work against each other.

It wasn't much Greg thought. It didn't look that significant on paper. But Greg knew that these actions had realigned Jiffy's culture and helped communicate it. The Execs role modelled the culture and rewarded it. Most of all the whole organisation told its own stories to reinforce the new culture in a virtuous cycle.

The Craftsmen no-longer chuckled with derision about Jim's golf meetings, the Execs no longer complained about each other. The Head Office, once a symbol of excess and unfairness was now the opposite, a story about moving in together and improved equality across departments and pay grades.

New stories took hold and perpetuated the culture. Reps joked about the Naked Salesman, Craftsmen acknowledged the Execs who stayed late to make pizza for them. Everyone remembers pulling together to make the toy shop order. Greg decided to tell Jim these stories first, the theory of how the culture changed could come later.

Chapter 11

A true Craftsman

Jim wouldn't be coming in Greg learned from Fiona. He'd died the day after he returned from his holiday. It seems Jim was getting in a quick round of golf alone before his scheduled meeting with the Execs at the factory. Fellow golfers found him collapsed on the course, presumed heart attack.

Everyone was devastated. The Execs allowed employees to take the day off if they wanted to, some preferred to stay and work to honour

Jim's legacy. Others took the time off to mourn, or just stayed at the office not working to share their grief with others around the coffee machine.

The coffee machine was a new one, a surprise from Susan who arranged to buy two fancy machines with a supply of high quality tea and coffee, one for each floor. The Execs had recently agreed that Jiffy could officially give notice to the Head Office landlord to terminate the lease. The cost saving was more than enough to pay for the coffee machines. Better coffee seemed little comfort now Susan thought, wishing that they had arrived on any other day but this one.

Brian put up an old picture of Jim in the lobby, adding a black ribbon across one corner of the frame. Some of the craftsmen made up a highly polished wooden plaque to go underneath it, with Jim's motto skillfully engraved in italics *"solid wood, made to specification in the spirit of a true craftsmen"*.

Greg couldn't help but wonder what would have happened if Jim had died a few months earlier. Jiffy would have been in a perilous position. At least now the company had a renewed sense of purpose, it was more cohesive and the culture replaced some of the magic that Jim had once brought with him as the plucky hardworking founder. Now Jiffy had a chance to get through this without Jim. As sad as it was to acknowledge.

Susan was the bearer of more bad news. Jim's will had been read and his estranged wife was set to inherit the majority shareholding of Jiffy. They had been separated for years, Greg learned from Brian. She had had enough of the all night shifts in the early days and the all weekend golf in the latter ones. It was amicable and so it appears Jim never troubled himself to change his will. Some of the other early Craftsmen held small stakes in the company, including Brian, but Jim's former wife now held more than three quarters of the shares. Susan confirmed that according to the company articles she was able to do whatever she pleased. The really bad part was that she was looking to sell the shares as soon as possible to whoever offered the best price. Her solicitor had told Susan to expect calls from potential buyers in the near future.

Jim was buried shortly afterwards. The factory closed for the funeral and everyone who could attend was there. Greg spotted Jim's estranged wife at the service but restrained from asking her about business, despite his curiosity about Jiffy's future and anxiety about a change in ownership. He managed to hold it together and offered a hardly audible "Sorry for your loss" in passing. He could hardly fathom that she now owned the company instead of poor old Jim, a true Craftsman.

As CFO and effective head of the company, now that the CEO had died and not yet been replaced, Susan fielded all of the calls from potential buyers and brokers. Jim's wife had instructed her to meet with the buyers and to make the data room available to enable the sale to progress as quickly as possible.

Months went by and day to day challenges kept everyone distracted from the potential sale. New orders came in and a few rush jobs had motivated the firm. Mike was sure to capitalise on the rush work by increasing margins.

Tim and the IT department did an amazing job working with the Designers to revamp the website and to create an online system whereby Jiffy's production capacity was advertised and utilised by other firms who were short on capacity. The Craftsmen were able to turn their hands to almost any project, replicating the work of others quickly and accurately to enable a flexible production capability, a modern embodiment of Jiffy's slogan on the old workshop doors 'Ready in a Jiffy'. This short notice batch work brought in amazing returns. Soon it became a new pillar of Jiffy's strategy.

The Execs were pleased with the continued turnaround, but were wary that Jiffy's success also made it an increasingly valuable and attractive takeover target. As the sales crept up, so did the data room requests and number of bidders. This dragged out the process and caused a few sleepless nights as the anxiety took its toll.

Chapter 12

The new boss

Greg met Marty for the first time during the 'socialization meeting', held in the conference room along with the other Execs. Susan introduced him as "Marty from TexCap", which was the shorthand for Texas Capital Inc. An investment company from Austin, Texas who specialised in buying small and medium sized companies and then flipping them for a profit later. Some called them turnaround gurus, others called them vultures.

Marty looked like he came out of a cartoon, he wore cowboy boots and a large belt buckle, which was working hard to restrain his bulk around the midriff. There was no stetson, but Greg was sure he owned one. He looked very out of place in the Jiffy factory.

After a round of introductions Marty began, "As I'm sure you've gathered by now, TexCap has bought a majority stake in JFF". Spoken in his assertive Texan drawl.
"We call it Jiffy" Susan gently intervened. Marty was caught off-guard by the interruption and then chuckled to himself. "Jiffy, ok...TexCap now owns most of Jiffy, and accordingly we are going to put a lot of effort into growing and developing this company. We ended up paying a higher price than we wanted and so now I've got to justify that expense to my superiors by earning an even higher return, and then some". Marty continued after a pause, letting his message sink in "That means I need you all to pull together and to help me position this company for growth. TexCap has appointed me as the new CEO, so now you all work for me".

Mike glanced at Susan, who nodded to confirm that what Marty said was true. The Execs saw and resigned themselves to the new situation. They'd worked so hard to make a change at Jiffy, to get the company back on the right road, but now it was at risk of being hijacked in a new direction. Greg thought of how Jim would feel about Marty and TexCap, he wasn't sure that he'd approve.

Marty explained that he'd spend the first few days getting to know the company first hand. He'd seen the accounts in the data room but wanted to walk the factory floor and meet some customers. Mike winced at this point but quickly recovered before Marty noticed.

Marty wasn't a fool, he could see the uncertainty and anxiousness in the eyes of his new team. He'd seen it half a dozen times before, each time he'd walked into a new company to turn it around. "They may not like me now", he thought, "but in six months they'll be pleased with the transformation".

The next day Marty invited Greg into the conference room. Marty had been having one on one meetings with all of the Execs and now it was Greg's turn. "Come on in sport" said Marty, "it's time you and I spent some time together to plan how we fix this place".

"I was under the impression it wasn't broken" Greg shot back, his emotion talking before his mind had a chance to regulate the message. "What I mean is" Greg tried to back-peddle "we've been running a turnaround programme of our own for the last quarter or two and it's really been paying off, I think we should stay the course".

Marty paused and then opened up slowly, leaning back in his chair "I get it Greg, I understand, this is your baby, you've done a fantastic job, I saw it in the numbers. Great upswings in P&L, margins up, costs down. That's why I want you to partner with me to make a success of TexCap's investment". Greg gave a false grin and decided to listen, he could see Marty had his own idea of how this turnaround was going to work and he wasn't going to receive appeals from him.

"I've turned-around plenty of companies, similar to this in fact, manufacturing, batch-lots, in-house design. TexCap has grown sales by an average of 150%, cut costs more than 20% and returned a hell of a lot to our investors". He went on sermonising "problem is, deal flow has dried up, US is saturated, so this is our first overseas expansion play". Greg gulped. "I need to show my colleagues at TexCap that we can take our know-how and experience and apply it in new markets. So your job, as COO, is to back me up. To implement the formula that's worked so many times before. Work with me on this and in less than a year you'll have a nice fat bonus cheque waiting for you".

Greg was dismissed, he left the conference room feeling dejected and hopeless. As the main shareholder TexCap was well within their right to make changes, he was powerless to object. He could quit, he pondered, but then dismissed the idea. He'd put too much into Jiffy to abandon the company, he'd not only be walking away from a motivating place to work, he'd miss the other Execs who he'd grown close to through their shared challenges. Even Brian's crusty exterior had melted during the culture change, he was now a central pillar and authentic role model for how Jiffy operated. "For now", Greg moaned to himself.

The following week Marty called a meeting, it wasn't the Monday Morning Meeting, which Susan asked Fiona to not invite Marty to, unless he specifically asked, it was on Wednesday. Mike was called back from a Sales conference and Greg noticed immediately that Brian wasn't invited. "Howdy team, let's get to work" Marty commanded "I've had the TexCap analysts back in Austin running some numbers and now I've got the necessary data we're able to take some action. We have a saying at TexCap 'Data driven decision making', the data does not lie" he repeated the last few words quietly, almost to himself only. As if out of habit.

"Firstly, I love the improved profits this team has delivered in the last few months, keep it coming, and more. I'm expecting a 20% improvement over last months numbers in the next quarter. Mike, that's with you, keep pushing margins, every penny counts" Marty continued. "One of the items we picked up was the inventory JFF holds is significantly more than industry standard coverage. Why do we hold so much?" Marty looked at Greg.

"Part of our business is about being reactive to short-term demand. 'We make it in a Jiffy' as our saying goes. We never know what type of material or how much of it we might need, so we overstock to be prepared" Greg explained.

"No dice" Marty ordered "it needs to be fixed, working capital needs to come down so inventory needs to be managed, fix it". Greg looked up and away, then wrote down his action to speak to Brian about it, "where was Brian?" He thought again.

Looking at Jane, Marty asked "Speaking of cash flow, another problem we have is payroll, it's very erratic, changing month to month, why are we varying pay cheques so much?"

"It's our incentive programme" Jane responded "Employees get a share of savings and extra margin, so we put it through payroll". Marty looked around like someone had made a joke.

"Extra margin goes to the employees?" He said flabbergasted.

"A share of it" Susan corrected "of all savings 5% goes into the employee fund and another 5% goes to the employee".

"Hmmm, employee fund huh" Marty considered. "What is that used for?"

"It depends on what we need" said Tim, who'd been quiet up to now "this year we can finally expect a decent Christmas party, because we have allocated some of the fund towards it"

"Who decides on allocating funds and this incentive programme?" Marty delved deeper.

"We do, the Executives" Mike answered. "We cover it in our weekly meeting". He knew he'd invited more questions by the time he finished his sentence.

"Ok", said Marty, "I can see there's some things that the data room didn't cover. Send me an invite for that meeting and I'll sit in next time. In the meantime no payments to employees and no allocations from the fund".

"Last item of business, people changes. You can see that Brian isn't here today, that's because he's not on the top team, we need to establish a bit more order here. Greg as COO, Brian now reports to you. Can't understand what your job was anyway without Brian reporting to you. Also he'll be moving out of his office onto a desk on the factory floor, better that way, more visible to the Operators, will help to keep them in line. "We call them Craftsmen, not Operators" Jane interjected. Marty glared at her.

"Also" Marty added, "Fiona will be leaving us. I don't need an Executive Assistant and we need to find payroll savings anyway".

Greg caught up with Brian after the meeting. "Can we find somewhere quiet to talk"

"Sure, let's use my office" Brian said.

"That's probably not a good idea, let's take a walk outside" Greg countered. As they walked Greg broke the bad news, Brian was going to lose his office and wasn't going to be part of the Executives. On the bright side he wasn't going to have to report to Marty, so Greg used that as a joke to break the tension. It didn't really work.

Brian was quiet, in deep thought. He was looking at the horizon when he finally spoke. "It kills me to see Jiffy take backward steps, I've done it before and I don't want to do it again." He paused then confessed more to Greg "When TexCap bought out Jiffy they made an offer to all of the other shareholders too, given the inflated valuation and my otherwise minimal retirement fund, I decided to take it. I'm never going to be a millionaire, my shareholding was modest at best, but it gives me options. I think my best option right now is to just walk away".

Greg was sad but understood. Brian left a few days later, after clearing out his office. His departure was described as retirement, but everyone seemed to know that Brian's misgivings about TexCap's investment was the real reason. The Execs threw a retirement party at a local pub and paid out of their own pockets for drinks and snacks, rather than using the Employee fund and disobey Marty. Marty wasn't invited.

Chapter 13

Don't mess with Texas

The following Monday was Marty's first time at the Monday Morning Meeting. He ran the agenda and Greg had to pick-up the slack from Fiona's departure, pulling the data together for the incentive plan and presenting the ideas. Tim had helped to automate as much as possible from the website but the hard copy suggestions still had to be transcribed.

"So this is the incentive programme?" Marty asked rhetorically. Greg put the first idea on the slideshow. "Set-up an apprenticeship scheme to bring in the next generation of Craftsmen" was the first item. Marty overruled immediately "We don't need more payroll cost, especially not if they won't be actually adding value immediately. We need to streamline and invest in mechanised capacity, that will speed up production and we can depreciate the investment cost over a long period, keeping the books healthy".

The other Execs looked at each other aghast. The statement was an insult to Jiffy. Jim really would be turning in his grave. Greg was pleased Brian wasn't in the meeting, he feared he would have punched Marty square in the face.

Greg moved to the next slide, with a mischievous smirk "Ask the Naked Salesman to show guests around at the next open day" Marty hit the roof.
"What the hell is this?! Some sort of joke?"
Greg agreed. "Yes, probably, a bit of fun, probably from the Craftsmen" Greg knew who it was, he'd transcribed the note himself onto

the slide, expecting to get a rise out of Marty. He did it for a reason, he wanted to demonstrate the Jiffy culture.

"We always accept and list every suggestion for the incentive programme" Greg outlined the system to Marty "Everyone knows that any idea could be a winner, or could be combined with another idea to be improved, so we don't censor them. In this case I'm sure the guys downstairs wanted to have a laugh at the bosses expense, probably a protest at Brian leaving".

Marty was literally red faced. Visibly controlling his words and trying not explode he said "Tell those Operators to stop crafting bullshit jokes and to focus on making money. I don't think you understand the pressure we're under to grow this business. This is supposedly an important Executive meeting, I don't want distractions like this again".

Greg decided against explaining the Naked Salesman story and moved on. "Third and last item this week, 'build our own pizza oven outside instead of hiring one for events'". The

Execs were nodding, it made sense. Marty let out a puff of air and took the team to school "You guys just don't get it do you? We need to save every penny, to cut back, not to spend more" Marty stood up and paced the room.

"I've been considering this since our meeting last week, I don't mind the incentive programme, I can see it's value, but we need to focus the efforts towards savings, not frivolous expenditure and jokes." Marty was cooling down now, speaking slower, but it could have been the pacing which was making him short of breath. "Also, I'm changing the structure of the scheme, we're going to do something really nice for our employees. Instead of cash payments, we're going to allot equity in the company. The amounts will be small overall, fractions of 1%, but making them stockholders will encourage them to grow the company in the long term." He wasn't to be reasoned with. Jane was charged with setting up the scheme and making arrangements for annual allotments of equity to employees whose contributions made savings for Jiffy.

The change in the incentive scheme was communicated to employees through email and verbally by Greg to the Craftsmen on the shopfloor, Brian hadn't been replaced and Marty was making noises that wanted to save payroll cost, so Greg was filling in as the Factory Manager for the foreseeable future. The Foremen gave him plenty of support. When advised about the change to the incentive plan there were a few raised eyebrows and plenty of muttering, but no one asked a question.

The following week Greg was preparing for the Monday Morning Meeting, his fear was realised when he reached into the suggestion box. Nothing. Empty. He checked the email inbox which was the same. After a few weeks of the same, Marty cancelled the Monday Morning Meeting. He didn't see the need to discuss routine matters across departments, he could direct from the top, leaving the Execs with more time to find improvements and optimisations.

Greg looked back over his notes. He wished he could have protected some of the changes he'd implemented, it seemed his culture change initiative was dying in adolescence. The incentive programme was broken, the Monday Morning Meeting cancelled. Craftsmen being treated as Operators and Marty was talking about investing in more machines. It had gone so wrong so quickly, he reflected.

Chapter 14

A story of failure

The machines arrived the next quarter. Craftsmen were trained to be Operators, a few lost their jobs. The machines could process and shape the wood more quickly and efficiently than the craftsmen, even if the finished article wasn't quite as good. The mood at the factory was solemn.

Sales were struggling and Mike was pushing his team harder to find margin. They complained about being undercut by competitors and losing credibility with their existing clients due to lower quality and jacked-up rates. Mike realised he was pushing Marty's message downward and he didn't like it. It was affecting the team. The Sales Reps had been forced to cut back on lunches and they blamed Mike for not protecting them.

Similarly, the Design team was in trouble. Marty asked Mike to outsource most of the work to an offshore provider who could do the work for a much better rate. There were a few Designers left at the factory, mostly coordinating with the offshore team, but it wasn't the same. It took too long and plenty got lost in translation.

Tim in IT was overloaded. He needed more people to keep the new machines up and running and to manage the automated capacity system that leased out Jiffy's capabilities online. Marty refused to grant him more funds. On the day the Christmas party was cancelled to save funds, he quit.

Marty knew things were heading South. He fought a rear-guard action to explain the downturn in profits to the team in Austin and doubled down on what he knew to fix things at Jiffy. Higher volumes, lower costs. "We need to push harder" he told Greg "I've done this before, eventually the market will adjust and we'll be market leaders, just like my old company, 'Lone Star Mill'".

Later Greg researched 'Lone Star Mill'. It seemed to be a TexCap investment that was bought, expanded and flipped for four times the value less than two years later. Greg kept reading and discovered what he suspected. Lone Star Mill was now broke. TexCap had pumped up the company, made the numbers look good and flipped it for a nice profit. Probably bagging some hefty bonuses for Marty and his peers. Greg ran to tell Susan and Mike the bad news.

Mike was talking to Marty about a rush job, his 'Naked Salesman' had continued in the Jiffy spirit and found a client with a short-term demand for 20,000 units. Marty was beaming and noticed Greg approach "You see Greg, this is what I'm talking about. Mike has found us a juicy batch job. It'll patch-up a sizeable hole in our P&L. Austin will be pleased"

"Great" said Greg, genuinely quite pleased to see new business coming in "I'll get the Designer and the duty Foreman together now to plan the run" he operated out of routine, the excitement building in him in expectation of another Jiffy legend. 20,000 units was going to be real push, but he knew they could do it.

But then it fell apart. The Designers couldn't work out the specification quickly enough, the job had come in during the afternoon and the team in the offshore office had already gone home due to the time difference. Furthermore the machinery took longer to calibrate for the new order than expected. Tim wasn't around to help the Operators and test run after test run failed to get the specification right.

Eventually the run was moving forward but then another snag, Jiffy didn't have the inventory. The warehouse was stipped bare, but it was no use, the run wouldn't be completed in time. More inventory would take days to be delivered and it would be too late. Greg was pulling his hair out, but inwardly felt vindicated. He knew Marty had destroyed the Jiffy culture, a culture that had been a source of inertia for the company, a binding and motivating force that steered everyone at Jiffy to achieve their recent success.

Now it was a burden. Worse, it was a source of failure. The Jiffy culture had become 'cut cost', 'data driven', 'short-term'. The new stories were of cancelled Christmas parties, old-hands like Brian and Tim leaving and of a 20,000 unit order going to waste.

Greg gave Susan the bad news about the order. She looked up from her desk with tears in her eyes, Greg tried to console her, not understanding the problem. "It's a problem but we can get past it, there'll be more orders…" he trailed off, realising it wasn't working. Susan looked up and said "We're not going to make payroll". Greg was shocked.
"How?" Greg asked. Susan continued.

"We spent a lot of cash on those machines. The bank wouldn't agree to the financing, they didn't agree with Marty's financial projections. Marty told us to push on anyway using cash, he also wanted to avoid the additional debt cost of taking outside finance. As our orders began to dry up our income fell radically. I asked TexCap for a bridge loan but they rejected on the basis of the fund rules; we're already at 100% of our capital allocation. That big order was going to save us, it would have helped us through some lean months, but now we're going broke". The shame of the words hit her as she muttered them, it hurt Susan professionally as a CFO and personally as a long-time employee at Jiffy. Next she went to see Marty and confirmed that the short runway had become a hole in the ground. Marty asked her to leave his office and Greg saw him pick-up the phone through the office window. He dialed a long number, probably Austin, Texas.

Epilogue

Revolution

Jiffy folded. There was no way around it. The administrators took control and did their best to salvage something for the creditors. Hearing them refer to the company as JFF was driving Susan mad, after asking them to call it Jiffy a few times she gave up.

Most of the staff got paid what they were owed for the days worked, but were then laid off. The machinery was sold, the lease on the factory cancelled. The coffee machines would go back to the supplier at a discounted rate. Susan and Mike made coffees for everyone on the last day to use up the coffee stocks and to say sorry for the shocking and sudden decline of Jiffy. The employees understood that the Execs were powerless to resist against TexCap. As major shareholder they were in a position to do whatever they wanted. Now TexCap was gone, their investment worthless. Marty flew home. No one said goodbye.

Brian invited the Execs to dinner at his house, Tim came too. Brian had heard all about the collapse of Jiffy from his friends who were still working there at the end. Everyone in the community knew someone at Jiffy so it was hard to escape the bad news. He thought they all needed some cheering up, so he ordered plenty of wine and fired up the pizza oven that he had recently built in the garden. After too much wine and plenty of moaning about TexCap the team were laughing and joking again.

The stories came out. How Marty had flipped when they suggested the Naked Salesman at the open day, the one about making terrible pizza during the rush job, how Greg had nearly torpedoed his career by describing Jim as 'asleep at the wheel' in his first few weeks. Poor Jim, they reflected. At least he didn't live to see his company die.

Brian wept openly, unashamed. He spoke through his tears "I worked night and day with Jim. Sweat with him. Suffered cuts and bruises with him. Even helped hire you lot" he joked at the end. "I can't see his memory be dishonoured this way." Brian cleared his throat and spoke more clearly. "I want to make a new Jiffy, to start it all again, will you join me?"

They all said yes. Brian put up some small seed capital, the other Execs joined him with what they could afford. It didn't require too much as they only needed to purchase a small number of machines and some initial inventory.The bank lent the rest after Susan used her good relationship and the Jiffy name (officially Jiffy now, rather than JFF) to convince them. Along with some believable financial projections.

The factory was leased back, the Craftsmen rehired. Slowly at first, but growing in numbers as the work came back. The Designers and Marketers returned at Mike's insistence. No offshoring, everything would be done at the factory. Tim set-up an even better website and digital ordering system. The incentive programme came back, along with Fiona to run it. The coffee machines were reinstalled. Tim volunteered to organise the first 'new Jiffy' Christmas party, it was a huge success. A new routine to be repeated.

Susan became CEO, she was replaced by Rebecca her long-time deputy, selected on her skill´ set, experience and her consistent Jiffy culture behaviour. Despite being the major shareholder Brian preferred it in the Factory and remained Factory Manager, reporting directly to Susan. Greg was in charge of putting every part of the old Jiffy culture back in its place. A strategic role that supported and complemented Sales, Marketing and Operations and was critical for employee engagement. Greg became CCO, Chief Culture Officer.

Afterword

The objective of this book is to show the reader that culture change is hard work, but that it can be done and done quickly. The beginnings of significant change are within grasp - culture is not so hard to change that change shouldn't be attempted. By learning from this story, by asking others in your organisation to read this book and by embracing the lessons of culture change 'in a Jiffy' readers can embark on their own culture change initiative.

The culture seminar that Greg refers to throughout the story is fictional, but reflects the broad range of culture change literature. Combining the theory with the author's own experiences of culture change provides a more comprehensive and practical parable that is more memorable and easily relatable for practitioners. The author encourages readers to explore the Culture, Change Management and Strategy literature further, with one request - to remember that culture change doesn't have to be complicated. Understand the organisation's beliefs, assess what needs to change and then quickly and proactively make adjustments to the rewards, rituals, structures and most of all stories of the organisation. These steps will go a long way to creating an effective culture change.

The story of Jiffy and the culture changes the company experience represent many of the typical cultural pressures enterprises everywhere have to contend with at some point or another. Be it management or organisation changes, influences from the external environment or the changing role of a charismatic founder. The tale of Greg, who first spends time discovering then seeking to actively direct the Jiffy culture demonstrates that culture can be changed proactively, rather than just letting it organically develop. In particular, Greg discovers that intangible and seemingly minor changes can have a significant cultural impact.

Organisational culture is a dynamic medium, some of its most powerful proponents are the stories people tell and the rituals they obey. Stories and rituals become embedded in the beliefs of the organisation. The goal of culture change is to understand and change these beliefs to suit the direction of the organisation. As the stories and rituals are passed on to new joiners so are the beliefs. The stories live on, even after the protagonists have left or moved departments. The morals and belief system reinforced by these stories do more to instruct and guide employees than the strategies and goals mandated by leaders. Stories last a long time. Strategies and goals change frequently. Humans are conditioned to listen, learn from and to repeat stories. Storytelling is the life-blood of culture.

The control and reward systems in an organisation give the culture some shape, a framework, a skeleton. The rules and conditions have to be consistent with the stories however, a reward programme that is counter to the culture, or is not consistently delivered may do more harm than good, encouraging the opposite behaviour than desired, or just plain disenfranchisement. The example of the crude jokes put into the suggestion box at Jiffy provide a scenario of this type of problem. If the Execs had withdrawn the suggestion and punished the employee then that would become a story in itself. The employees would be more careful about what they submitted by self censoring. The jokes would be restrained, but the wacky and more creative ideas would probably get lost too. The suggestions would have been less forthcoming if there was a chance of punishment or reprisal ingrained in the system.

Control systems and incentives correct behaviours, like guardrails, pulling abnormal behaviour back from the brink and giving an instruction to do it differently. If someone does something seriously in breach of the culture they are often excommunicated. They are shunned and less respected, continued disobedience results in them either leaving or being fired, which in turn becomes a story about what not to do. A culture can be fragile, heavy handed leaders can damage the culture easily, by saying the wrong thing or acting the wrong way.

The introduction of Marty, and the sudden change in culture which inevitably leads to the failure and rebirth of Jiffy, shows the powerful role leaders play in shepherding culture. Not only are leaders watched and their actions taken as examples of how to behave, the leader controls the incentives and punishments. Leaders set the organisation design and have control over the symbols of the culture, likes offices, product lines, brands and events.

Texas Capital's investment in Jiffy also portrays the increasingly common national culture clash, whereby the culture of the firm is overlaid with the home country cultural traits of the actors in the organisation. In the case of Jiffy it is quite one-sided, however in multinational companies, the melting pot of nationalities in the workforce combined with a global network of offices and sub-offices creates a new level of complexity. Even in the case of Jiffy, the Factory and the Head Office had different cultures in the beginning, due to the different actions of their leaders, their routines and rituals and of course the stories they told themselves about their own sub-group (Head Office or Factory) and also about the other group.

Greg's vindication and the future success of Jiffy is a testament to a growing awareness of culture amongst leaders and leading organisations. These organisations know that their culture is a secret sauce, a bit of magic that they can't quite grasp but which drives their success. The leaders in these organisations have been taught or have learned through socialisation and established norms how to behave, which in turn sets the right example and reinforces the culture. New leaders and employees get told the stories that resonate with the culture. Executives know how to pick and support the right stories to exemplify the culture and to spread it like a positive virus.

It is important to acknowledge that Jiffy's particular challenges were mainly in Marketing, specifically the type of products they produced and their customer mix. These problems stemmed from strategic decisions that evolved over time and led the company into a competitive dead-end. The change in culture went a long way to correcting the strategy and in turn the competitiveness of Jiffy. But of course every company has different challenges, sometimes the culture needs to change in terms of Operational Efficiency, Sales Technique or in Safety. The key is to design and aspire to a culture that fits the value drivers of the company, ideally whilst respecting the company's legacy.

Furthermore the business of Jiffy is manufacturing goods from timber, a business and industry selected to be purposefully simplistic. Stewarding culture doesn't only apply to high-tech firms and new fast-moving internet companies. Culture is everywhere, every company, every office, every charitable organisation and every public body. Leaders in all of these organisations need to assess, understand and proactively manage the culture of their organisation.

Many companies have a prescribed culture, a set of standards and expected behaviours. But they are often underutilised and not referred to in daily practice. The habit at Jiffy of repeating the mottos (old and new), using them to guide discussions and having the motto prominently displayed as a prompt should be more commonplace. But most of all leadership needs to take control of the culture. To understand what is says about the company now and to craft what culture they need to survive and thrive. Only then can the organisation be built around that culture and the incentives tailored to encourage culture supporting behaviour. By knowing which behaviours to promote and which values to advocate leaders know what stories to reinforce, encouraging others to live the culture.

The author has taken some poetic licence with company name Jiffy and the double meaning it has for speed. Changing culture 'in a jiffy' may seem misleading, we know that culture takes time to solidify. Stories travel slowly and human nature is skeptical of change until we see the evidence that it is beneficial before we willingly adapt. However the steps Greg took to change the culture at Jiffy were relatively quick. Changing the incentives, moving the office, these were bold first moves that were established in weeks, not years. Clearly the actions at Jiffy are fictional, however it is not beyond the bounds of reason to expect similar changes to be implemented in real life by a determined leader, especially in smaller organisations. While the culture began to change, 'in a jiffy', the stabilization and proliferation of the culture took more time. But again the expectation is of change over a period of weeks and months, rather than years. Culture change in a jiffy is obtainable, even if it is only the initial culture change steps of a longer journey. The beginnings of a culture change programme start as soon as a leader announces it, by setting new expectations, role-modelling and rewarding different behaviours and telling new stories.

An organisation's culture is changing constantly with each deed, each message and each new product and customer. The changes are slight, but there is constant evolution. In addition leaders must remember that cultures are not uniform, there are 'pockets' and subcultures that will have developed in different buildings, business units and product lines. Current and previous leaders in the organisation will have influenced the cultures within their own teams. A culture change initiative should seek out these differences and understand them. Accordingly, the starting point for each 'pocket' is different and so the new rituals, routines and stories may be different for each team or business unit. A different illness will require a different medicine.

Changing culture is a craft. It requires a sense of what materials you have to work with and what you want to make in the end. A skilled craftsman (or craftswoman) knows which tools to use to change the material and understands that one false move can ruin the end result. The craftsman uses knowledge and experience to make the right changes. The more skilled the craftsman, the quicker the change and the better the result. An operator uses a 'cookie cutter' approach. Uses the same old methods, repeats the same design, uses a machine to repeat the process without deviation. Marty was an operator. Greg and the Execs were craftsmen. Use the lessons of this story to be a culture craftsman.

32891129R00070

Printed in Great Britain
by Amazon